There is someone for everyone

Atheneum Books for Young Readers
An imprint of Simon & Schuster Children's Publishing Division
1230 Avenue of the Americas
New York, New York 10020

Book design by Ann Bobco

The text of this book is set in Deepdene.
The illustrations are rendered in watercolor.

Printed in Hong Kong
2 4 6 8 10 9 7 5 3 1

Library of Congress Cataloging-in-Publication Data
Mathers, Petra.
Dodo gets married / by Petra Mathers. — 1st ed.
p.   cm.
"An Anne Schwartz Book"
Summary: Dodo, an exotic German bird, befriends a one-legged retired sea captain and marries him.
ISBN 0-689-83018-1
[1. Dodo—Fiction. 2. Weddings—Fiction.] I. Title.
PZ7.M42475 Do 2001
[E]—dc21   99-086369

FIRST
EDITION

Dodo Gets Married

by petra mathers

An Anne Schwartz Book

ATHENEUM BOOKS FOR YOUNG READERS

New York London Toronto Sydney Singapore

Every Saturday Dodo rode past Captain Vince's house on her way home from the market.

I just love zese little windmills, she always thought.
But zat poor captain in zere, such a sad story.

There's that German gal from Crook Road again, thought the captain. Always gawking and sticking her beak over the hedge.

Captain Vince used to fly a helicopter for the Coast Guard, until he lost a leg in a dangerous rescue mission.

He missed flying, and he missed his friends, but when they called,
he didn't answer the phone. They're just feeling sorry for me, he thought.

One Saturday Dodo couldn't help herself
and stopped for a closer look.
"Just look at zem go round and round,"
she said.

"There's nothing for sale here," the captain
grumbled.
"How nice to meet you," cried Dodo.
"You're such an artist."

"Ach, but now it is raining.
I don't like ze drops dropping on me."
"You can wait it out in the shed if you
want," said the captain.

Zis is cozy, Dodo thought, settling in.
Vince was watching her from his window.
What the heck is she doing? he wondered.

"Yoo-hoo, Captain, I see you!" cried Dodo. "Come have some lunch."

"I'll make you my papa's special seaweed sandwich. He was a captain, too."

"You should have heard his stories.
Sea monsters, pirates, flying cheeses."

"But my favorite was How Papa Got His
Glass Eye. He'd always tell it different—
sometimes scary, sometimes sad, and once
I laughed so hard I fell off his lap."

"Welcome back sun, and we have eaten all ze shopping!" said Dodo.
"Now you have room in your basket," said the captain.

"See you Saturday, Captain, and I am sorry about your leg. Did you notice it squeaks a little?"

That night Captain Vince had only one thing on his mind.

Dodo was too happy to go to bed. "Good night, little windmill," she whispered. "Don't be scared, I'll be right inside."

By summertime Vince and Dodo had become best friends.
One morning Dodo heard a helicopter.

"Why, it's Vince's old chopper!" she cried.
"Heaven above, somezing is coming down!"

"What's going on?" Vince's friends wondered.

"I don't know, looks like she's running away," Vince groaned.

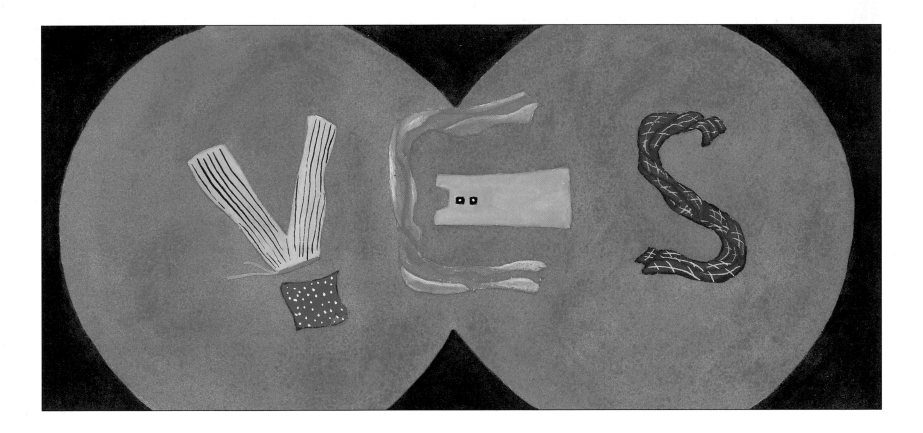

He took another look.
"I'll be a monkey's uncle," he cried.
"She loves me!"

The very next day Dodo and her friends Lottie and Herbie drove across
Moose Bay Bridge to the wedding store.

"Come in, come in, brrides and grrooms, who is the lucky one?" asked Miss Annabell.

It was not easy to find a dress in Dodo's size.

Herbie dawdled choosing the little figures for the top of the cake. They looked like candy.

"Sir, our brrides and grrooms are not edible," said Miss Annabell.

There was a lot to do to get ready for the wedding. Herbie was in charge of the outside decorations.

The summer heat was fierce. Even the cake was sweating.

The night before the
wedding Dodo took a
beauty bath.

Something went terribly
wrong.

After hours of scrubbing,
she gave up.

When she turned off the light, Dodo glowed. "Ze poor Vince," she sobbed. "He wants a pink wife but gets a green one, and at night she turns into a lamp."

When it was time to get married, Dodo covered herself from head to toe. She was so hot she could hardly breathe.

"Dodo darling, how green you are!" Vince cried.

"She's coming to," said Lottie.
"Somezing in ze tub," Dodo whispered.
"I'm green all over, and I glow in ze dark."

"My sunshine, my night-light, hold on to me," said Vince.

The wedding was lovely, the cake was delicious.

The sun set, the moon rose. It was a glorious day on Crook Road.

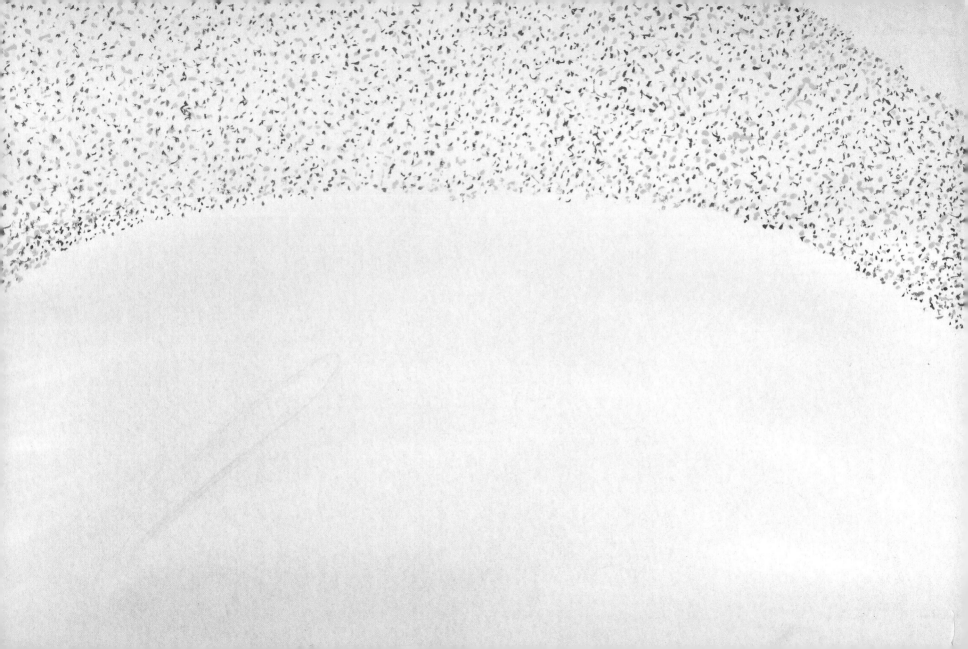